SANFORD'S SYNOPSIS OF LIBEL AND PRIVACY

by Bruce W. Sanford

WORLD ALMANAC BOOKS
An imprint of Funk & Wagnalls Corporation

Copyright © 1991 by Bruce W. Sanford

All rights reserved. No part of this book may be reproduced in any form or by any means without permission in writing from the publisher.

First published in 1977.
Revised edition published in 1981, 1984, and 1991

Library of Congress Catalog Number: 80-85391
ISBN 0-88687-649-4

Copies of this book are available at special discounts on bulk purchases. For more information, please contact the Sales Department, World Almanac Books, 1 International Blvd., Mahwah, NJ 07495.

Printed in the United States of America

Cover design: Nancy Carey
Interior design: Charles Sutherland

World Almanac Books
An imprint of Funk & Wagnalls Corporation
1 International Blvd.
Mahwah, NJ 07495
(201) 529-6900

10 9 8 7 6

CONTENTS

FOREWORD 1
HOW TO AVOID LIBEL AND INVASION OF PRIVACY LAWSUITS 3
THE LAW OF LIBEL 5
  Introduction 5
  The Elements of Libel 7
  Who's Public? Who's Private? 10
    The Most Litigious People 12
  Quoting Libel 13
  Common Types of Libel 14
    Publishing Pitfalls 14
    Broadcasting Bloopers 15
  Defenses 15
    In General 15
    Truth 16
    Privilege 16
    Opinion and Fair Comment 17
    Consent 19
    The Right of Reply 19
    Statute of Limitations 20
  Mitigating Circumstances 20
    In general 21
    Retraction 21
    Mistaken Identity 22
    Provocation 22
    Bad Character of Plaintiff 23
    The "Libel-proof" Defense 23
  Protecting Confidential Sources 23
    Sources and Newsroom Discussions 23
    Notes and Memos: Record Retention 25
INVASION OF PRIVACY 26
  In General 26
  The Right of Privacy 27
  Defenses 29
  Mitigation 31
"RED FLAG" WORDS 32
ABOUT THE AUTHOR 35

FOREWORD

LIBEL AND PRIVACY IN THE 1990s: GROWTH INDUSTRIES

Many people who make up juries don't like the news media. They think reporters are chronically careless with the facts and cavalier with people's reputations and private lives.

Throughout the 1980s, many of these jurors expressed their resentment by awarding staggering damages to plaintiffs in libel and invasion of privacy lawsuits. Plaintiffs like Brown & Williamson, Wayne Newton and a Philadelphia D.A. have won multi-million dollar jury verdicts.

Accordingly, this work, like earlier editions, is pragmatic. It is designed to alert journalists to the dangers of libel and invasion of privacy and help prevent serious lawsuits from arising.

This thin volume deals with bodies of law at once ancient and young. Born centuries ago, the law of libel has undergone the most major mutations in its history during the past twenty five years. The changes have been the handiwork of the U.S. Supreme Court, which has 'constitutionalized' the old common law of libel.

Similarly, the law of invasion of privacy, a twentieth-century tort, has grown tremendously in the past few decades. This growth has undoubtedly been nurtured by a popular notion that Americans must shelter themselves from intrusions of the mass media into their private lives. There are few signs that this growth will abate in the foreseeable future, although the news media surely will resist vigorously all attempts to limit news coverage and the public's right to receive information about human events as well as public affairs.

The new directions of libel law are clearer than those of privacy law. Since 1964, the Supreme Court has struggled to find a reasonable accommodation between the First Amendment interest in uninhibited, robust press coverage of public affairs and a state's legitimate interest in compensating individuals for injury to reputation. The struggle began with the Court's landmark decision in *New York Times Co. v. Sullivan*, which ruled that a public official could not recover damages for libel without proof that the libel had been published with deliberate knowledge of its falsity or with reckless disregard of the truth. This so-called *New York Times* rule presented public officials with a new, onerous burden of proof. In 1967, the applicability of the *New York Times* rule was expanded to apply not only to public officials but also to public figures.

In 1974, however, the Court decided that private individuals (and that might include people of some prominence) should have an easier burden than public people to recover for libel. In *Gertz v. Robert Welch, Inc.*, the Court said that the plaintiff, a well-known Chicago lawyer appearing in a criminal case of great public interest, could recover for false statements upon proving mere negligence in the preparation and writing of a story. The Court invited each of the fifty states to set its own standards of liability when a private individual sues for libel. In 1976, and again in 1979, the Court handed down rulings restricting rather than expanding the definition of who is a 'public figure' for purposes of libel law.

The 1980s saw a rainstorm of libel cases, starting with Carol Burnett's $1.3 million verdict against *The National Enquirer*. By the end of the decade, a trio of Supreme Court decisions had stabilized the law, but some successful libel plaintiffs had also shown that the press could not expect to win every case under the modern, more favorable law. Importantly, a new generation of justices like Justice Sandra Day O'Connor and Justice John Paul Stevens had signed on to the central premise of the bold new American constitutional law given us in 1964 by Justice William J. Brennan, Jr.

This synopsis covers only the broad general principles of libel and the right of privacy and is not intended as an exhaustive legal treatise. Specific problems invariably involve individual considerations and should be promptly referred to legal counsel.

HOW TO AVOID LIBEL AND INVASION OF PRIVACY LAWSUITS

1. Avoid slipshod, indifferent or careless reporting. Whenever a statement could injure someone's reputation, treat it like fire. The facts of a story should be confirmed and verified, as far as practicable, in accordance with customary professional procedures.

2. Truth is a defense, but there may be a vast difference between what's true and what can be proved to be true to a jury. When in doubt whether a story is accurate, check it out. Remember, a retraction is not a complete defense to a libel action but serves merely to mitigate or lessen damages.

3. There is no wholesale exemption from libel for anything that might be labeled opinion. If a statement reasonably implies false facts about someone, be prepared to defend the statement. Base criticism or commentary on facts that are fully stated and accurate.

4. Watch out for the "routine" story of minor significance. It frequently doesn't get enough editorial attention and, probably for that reason, accounts for more libel cases than all of the investigative reporting and human interest stories combined. Make reports of arrests, investigations and other judicial or legislative proceedings and records precise and accurate.

5. Try to get "the other side of the story." A good reporter sticks to the facts and not to some bystander's opinion of what might be the truth if the facts were known.

6. Take particular care with quotations. The fact that a person is quoted accurately is not necessarily a defense to a libel action if the quoted statement contains false information about someone.

7. Never "railroad" a story through; edit it carefully to make sure it says precisely what you want it to say. Don't use sly or cute innuendo to suggest some misbehavior that you don't describe explicitly. If you're going to attack someone or injure someone's reputation, do it right.

8. Avoid borderline cases of invasion of privacy since the law of the right of privacy is still developing. Egregious insensitivity to the tender and non-newsworthy parts of a person's life may earn you only the wrath of a jury.

9. Don't use unauthorized names and pictures for advertising or other commercial purposes. Don't use unidentified pictures to illustrate social or other conditions when pictures of people who expressly consent, including professional models or staff members, will suffice and are readily obtainable.

10. If an error has been made, always handle demands for retractions that come from a lawyer for a potential plaintiff with the advice of legal counsel. A well-meaning but unnecessary or poorly worded correction may actually prejudice a publisher's or broadcaster's defenses in a subsequent lawsuit.

THE LAW OF LIBEL

INTRODUCTION

Every publisher or broadcaster would like to have a sure method of preventing libelous matter from getting into the columns of his newspaper or into his newscasts. Doubtless, if it can be assured that every statement carried by the paper or station is probably true (or substantially true, so that any variation or omission is immaterial), there will be a defense to any action for libel, although even then libel suits may be filed against the newspaper or station which must then be defended.

The duty every newspaper or broadcast station owes to its community is to report the news, but that duty carries with it the legal obligation not to interfere with the rights of others. The law has recognized for centuries that every person has a right to have the estimation in which he stands in the opinion of others unaffected by false statements to his discredit. Thus, the common law of this country, inherited from England, protects every person from the publication, *i.e.*, the dissemination, of libelous and slanderous statements to third persons.

The law of defamation is divided into two branches: *slander*, which consists of oral communication, and *libel*, which consists of printed or broadcast communication. A short general definition of libel may be given as follows:

A libel is a false statement printed or broadcast about a person which tends to bring that person into public hatred, contempt, or ridicule or to injure him in his business or occupation.

Libel law varies in each state, although federal constitutional law prevents a state from imposing liability upon a publisher or broadcaster for libel without a showing of falsity and some degree of fault. Within this boundary, and certain others for public personages, states determine for themselves what a plaintiff in a libel suit must prove and what defenses are available to a publisher or broadcaster. State laws also determine whether there may be prosecutions for criminal libel. Such prosecutions are rare, but since they are based upon the theory that the libel has disturbed the peace, they are punishable by fine or imprisonment. Civil libel, which gives rise to a cause of action by a person for damages, covers the experience of most journalists, and it is this branch of the law of libel that is addressed in this synopsis.

Three points about the scope of this work should be made. First, this book discusses libel law only as it applies to the news media. Libels published by persons through such media as letters, handbills or employment records may involve other considerations not discussed here. Vetting books for libel involves special considerations (in part because retracting mistakes is not nearly as easy as in daily journalism), but the rules of libel and privacy discussed here should help the author and book editor understand how to avoid problems.

Second, all working journalists should realize that the rules discussed in this work apply to them personally as employees of a newspaper or broadcast station. Reporters and editors responsible for writing or editing a libelous story are often named as additional defendants in a libel suit against a news media organization. It is the error of such employees that may make the organization liable for damages to the plaintiff, but such employees may also be held separately and personally liable for the libelous statements. Thus, although this book speaks of the liability of a newspaper or broadcaster, it should be remembered that the individual's liability may be identical.

Finally, the differences among state libel laws make it virtually impossible to generalize about many rules of libel law. *This book construes ambiguities or variations in the law against publishers or broadcasters.* Courts may, and indeed often will, interpret the law more favorably to the media, but **prudence dictates that this volume of preventive medicine be reasonably sour and startling rather than cherry-flavored.**

THE ELEMENTS OF LIBEL

Perhaps the simplest way to understand modern libel law — and to be able to assess the risks of any particular libelous statement — is to understand what a person has to prove in a libel lawsuit in order to recover damages.

What he has to prove depends largely upon who he is: a public official, public figure or private individual.

However, any plaintiff in a libel case, regardless of his status, has to establish the following elements:

1. **Publication,** i.e., that the statement was communicated to others. This element is easily established where a newspaper or broadcast story is involved.

2. **Identification,** i.e., that the statement was reasonably understood by people who knew the plaintiff as referring to him. Obviously, the plaintiff doesn't have to be specifically named to be identifiable. For example, ascertainable members of a group such as a school board can be identified by the description of an event, such as a fistfight between two boys.

3. **Falsity,** i.e., that people reasonably understood that a specific false statement of fact was made by the communication.

4. **Damages,** i.e., that the statement caused provable "actual injury," in the form of out-of-pocket losses, impairment of reputation, or mental anguish and suffering. Under common law, and until recently, such damages could be presumed or implied from the very fact that a libelous statement had been made.

The U.S. Supreme Court held in 1974, however, that neither presumed nor punitive damages are allowable unless the plaintiff proves that the publisher or broadcaster made the statement knowing that it was false or entertaining serious doubts as to its truth. Nevertheless, a jury has ample opportunity to punish a member of the media with an enormous verdict by finding "actual injury" in the form of mental anguish.

As recently as the 1960s, libel verdicts rarely exceeded $20,000. During the last decade, however, record-breaking verdicts have been returned with sobering frequency. The "typical" verdict nowadays exceeds six figures, as exemplified by these actual jury awards, some of which were reduced or reversed on appeal:

AWARD	ALLEGED FALSITY
$460,000	Article asserted college football coach had "fixed" a football game.
$3,000,000	Broadcast commentary accused tobacco company of targeting cigarette advertising toward teenagers.
$275,000	Article evaluated prosecutor's performance critically and unfairly.
$100,000	Report that socially prominent figure had been granted divorce because of "adultery" was technically inaccurate, although divorce trial testimony did contain sufficient evidence of extramarital conduct by both parties to "make Dr. Freud's hair curl," according to the trial judge.
$800,000	Article claimed that husband and wife were divorced and wife had a "reunion" in Las Vegas with Elvis Presley.
$7,000,000	Article characterized motel owner as a drug dealer.
$34,000,000	Articles reported that prosecutor had quashed charges against two college students, one of whom was his son's friend.
$4,560,000	Articles reported that police and prosecutor behaved improperly in prosecution of murder case.

5. **Fault.** The fifth and final element of a plaintiff's libel case is fault, usually the most crucial element. It is here that the plaintiff's status determines what must be proved.

If the plaintiff is a public official or public figure complaining about a statement related to his or her public role in life, then he or she must prove that the publisher or broadcaster made the statement either **knowing it was false or entertaining serious doubts as to its truth.** (This test is known as "actual malice," an unfortunate term since the test usually has nothing to do with malice in the sense of ill will or spite.)

If, on the other hand, the plaintiff is a private individual, then he or she may need to prove only that the publisher or broadcaster acted **negligently in failing to ascertain that the statement was false and that it defamed him or her.**

Thus, private individuals generally have a less severe burden of proof in a libel case than public officials or public figures. It may not be difficult, for example, for a surgeon to prove that a newspaper acted negligently in publishing reports that falsely accused him of embezzling hospital funds. A jury might find that the newspaper should not have relied on its sources or should have investigated the story more thoroughly.

If the surgeon were also a city councilman, however, he would probably have more difficulty proving his case. As a public official, he would have to show that the newspaper published the reports knowing they were false or entertaining serious doubts as to their truth. Proof of a mere failure to investigate would not suffice in this case. Rather, he would at least have to show that the newspaper acted with a reckless disregard for the truth by being aware of the probable falsity of the story but printing it anyway.

The concept of "fault" — be it negligence, recklessness, or deliberate falsehood — is one added to the common law in the past two decades by landmark decisions of the U.S. Supreme Court. The decisions have extensively revised the law of libel but have brought some uncertainty into the law.

No one knows, for instance, how much or what kind of "negligence" on a reporter's part is sufficient to make the reporter and his employer liable for a story that injures a private individual's reputation. In each case, a jury would be asked to determine whether the reporter acted reasonably or professionally in checking on the truth or falsity of the story prior to publication. A jury's opinion may well be different from a reporter's, especially in hindsight.

Likewise, public officials have won cases where they showed that a news story contained a contradiction on its face but the reporter didn't bother to make an obvious phone call that could have easily cleared up the matter. That sort of conduct — coupled with evidence of bias against the plaintiff — has been viewed as suggesting that the newspaper was reckless in handling the story.

The practical answer, therefore, is stark and simple: A reporter should handle with care and caution every story, especially one that tends to injure a person's reputation.

WHO'S PUBLIC? WHO'S PRIVATE?

One of the fundamental questions in a libel case is whether the plaintiff is a "public official" or "public figure," as opposed to a "private individual." Unfortunately, courts have not provided a reliable crystal ball.

The U.S. Supreme Court has consistently advised that the "public official" category does not encompass all public employees. Rather, it includes those government employees who have, or appear to the public to have, substantial responsibility for the conduct of governmental affairs. Thus, elected officials, political candidates, police officers, and judges are routinely

PUBLIC OFFICIAL
County medical examiner
High school chemistry teacher
Taxicab inspector
Recreation supervisor
Psychiatrist at state hospital
NON-PUBLIC OFFICIAL
Court-appointed attorney
High school history teacher
Undercover police informant
Government contractor conducting environmental impact analysis
Former governor

held to be "public officials." The list in the box on the previous page, however, illustrates the often differing results reached by courts that have considered the "public official" issue.

Even greater inconsistency pervades the "public figure" category. The Supreme Court has defined two general kinds of public figures:

a. Those persons who "occupy positions of such pervasive power and influence that they are deemed public figures for all purposes" (e.g., William F. Buckley, Jr., or Johnny Carson).

b. Those otherwise private individuals who have voluntarily thrust themselves into the vortex of a significant public controversy in order to influence the resolution of the issues involved (e.g., a vociferous opponent of a school bond levy).

In short, the determination is always a factual one. Many celebrities, socialites, entertainers, sports figures and other prominent people may not have sufficient "pervasive power and influence" to fall within the first group. And in the second group the existence of a substantial political or social controversy — whether local or national— may be necessary.

Whenever the question arises of whether a particular person is a public figure, it may be useful to consider these variables:

a. Does the person have access to the media to rebut any accusations?

b. What is the extent of the person's voluntary association with the limelight or a particular public controversy?

c. Does a genuine "public controversy" already exist or has it been created by the publisher or broadcaster?

What the public figure test lacks in precision or predictability, it makes up in flexibility. Nonetheless, the frustration factor is high. One judge has complained that "defining public figures is much like trying to nail a jellyfish to the wall." The following list should provide some sense of the results in a few actual cases:

PUBLIC FIGURES—"PERVASIVE POWER AND INFLUENCE"
James Earl Ray, convicted murderer of Dr. Martin Luther King Dr. Robert Atkins, author of diet books Wally Butts, college football coach Children of Julius and Ethel Rosenberg Bebe Rebozo, adviser to Richard Nixon Church with 5 million members
PUBLIC FIGURES—PARTICIPATION IN "PUBLIC CONTROVERSY"
Drug abuse foundation Insurance company Labor union Newspaper publisher Opponent of fluoridation Organized crime official President of consumer cooperative Professional and college athletes Retail meat company Sportswriter
NON-PUBLIC FIGURES
Criminal defendant Department store Ex-convict Fundraiser for a charity Harness race jockey Major stockholder in a large shopping mall Politically active attorney Research scientist on a government grant Resort corporation Wife of prominent industrialist

The Most Litigious People

Some categories of people seem to sue more than others. Certainly, as a group, prosecutors and former prosecutors seem to be the most winning libel plaintiffs. Other common types include: police, school officials, and doctors. Under the last category falls the most ironic libel lawsuit: the claim brought by Frank Sinatra's lawyer, Mickey Rudin, against Dow Jones' *Barron's*, for terming Rudin "Sinatra's mouthpiece." Dow Jones won.

QUOTING LIBEL

Elusive as the public person determination may be, it frequently doesn't matter prior to publication or broadcast whether a person is labeled public or private. After all, no professional reporter sits down at a typewriter, terminal, or videotape editing machine and says, "Well, this person is a public figure so I've got greater latitude to libel him." Good reporters focus on "getting it right," not on their margin for error.

Nevertheless, there is one area of reporting permeated by the public-private dichotomy. It involves the most common misconception about libel law: quoting libel. Many reporters believe they can avoid liability for a false statement so long as they merely repeat or attribute the statement to a particular person. The law is not that simple.

When public people are hurling accusations or epithets at each other — as is common during political contests or corporate takeover wars — a reporter is unlikely to be in a position to divine the truth or falsity of the charge. Typically, it is important to report the accusation simply because it was made. Under a variety of legal theories, most states recognize a privilege for the press to report such charges with impunity so long as the reporter does not espouse or endorse the truth of the charges but merely reports them accurately and neutrally.

Contrast the mudslinging of public people, however, with unsubstantiated gossip-mongering by private individuals. Say a neighbor tells you that an explosion next door happened because of the homeowner's "collaboration with a neo-Nazi group" or because the homeowner was "freebasing cocaine." Publishing or broadcasting that accusatory speculation, even with attribution, is playing with fire unless it can be substantiated by other sources or the police. If the accusation was false (say the explosion was actually caused by a faulty microwave oven), the homeowner might well sue both the neighbor (for slander) and the publisher or broadcaster (for libel). In that instance, the first four elements of a plaintiff's case (i.e., publication, identification, falsity, and damages) would be established easily and the verdict could turn on whether the reporter had acted unreasonably or unprofessionally in repeating the accusation.

COMMON TYPES OF LIBEL

There is no such thing as a "garden variety" libel. The kinds of libelous statements are as infinite as people's capacity to invent new ways to accuse, humiliate or disgrace others.

One characteristic does unify most species of libel: **potential injury to reputation.** Whenever a word, story, picture, caption, headline, lead-in or combination thereof can potentially injure someone's reputation, the warning bells and sirens inside an editor's or reporter's head should go off.

Publishing pitfalls

Any survey of libel litigation over the last several decades would indicate that certain areas in print journalism have been fertile territory for libel lawsuits. Some of these common problem areas include:

a. **False statements about criminal justice** — i.e., false reports of arrests, indictments, convictions, and prior criminal records. Easily the greatest number of cases fall in this category.

b. **False statements about children or professionals.** Parents jealously guard their children's reputations, and lawyers, teachers, doctors, and other people who trade on their reputations often feel they have no alternative but to file suit when a false statement has ruined their business or professional life.

c. **False headlines or "leads" that have been hyped** — they promised more than the full story delivered. In most states, many a lurid headline has been saved by the rule that a head must be read in conjunction with the full story, but hyped heads can still provoke years of nasty litigation.

d. **False rewrites, summaries, and condensations,** especially if handled by more than one rewrite person. It may be the "too-many-cooks" syndrome, but with depressing frequency the owner of a horse, accurately identified in the first story, becomes the suspended drugger of a horse in a later version. Or the victim of a crime becomes the perpetrator. Or, in copy editing, the phrase "a drug addiction problem" becomes "his" drug addiction problem.

Broadcasting bloopers

Television has its own special occasions for generating libel. Inaccurate, sloppy reporting still accounts for most lawsuits in broadcasting, as in print, but common problem areas unique to the electronic media include:

a. **False impressions from the use of generics or file footage,** the terms used to describe the typical street or crowd scene used to illustrate visually a voice-over narrative. Badly timed synchronization of the voiceover with the video may have a shopper being accused of shoplifting or a passerby on a street being accused of prostitution.

b. **False "promos," "teasers," "bumpers," "tosses," and all manner of other devices used to promote a program or maintain audience interest during commercial breaks.** The trouble usually stems from the need to advertise and summarize an upcoming segment. The opportunity for hype amounting to falsity is all too apparent.

c. **Breaking news on television presents unique problems because of the medium's immediacy.** Where injury to reputation is apparent from the nature of the breaking story (i.e., arrest of rape suspect), on-air reporters should be careful not to jump to conclusions or reach further than the facts of the moment justify.

DEFENSES

In general

Libelous material can be published or broadcast with reduced risk if it is covered by one of these defenses: (1) truth, (2) privilege, (3) opinion or fair comment, (4) consent, or (5) reply.

Most of these defenses were established by the common law long before the U.S. Supreme Court injected the concept of "fault" into libel law. The effect of the Supreme Court's decisions upon these defenses remains somewhat unresolved. State laws will evolve, probably differently, in this area during the years ahead.

Truth

The best defense to a libel suit is that the statement complained of is true (or substantially true, so that any variation or omission is immaterial). Generally speaking, truth is a complete defense — it will totally bar the plaintiff from recovery.

Therefore, the best safeguard against a libel suit is to make certain before publication that any potentially libelous statement is true and, even more importantly, can be proved true. The plaintiff, of course, bears the burden of proving that a statement about him or her is false, but as a practical matter, it's often critical to a successful defense effort to be able to prove truth.

Privilege

A privileged communication is one that would be libelous, under normal circumstances, but the occasion on which it is made allows the statement to be made without penalty. The privilege is granted on the theory that the interest of the individual being libeled is outweighed by the public interest in the proceeding or occasion on which the statement was made.

Thus, newspapers and broadcasters are entitled to defend a libelous statement on the grounds that the statement is conditionally or qualifiedly privileged. The extent of a qualified privilege varies greatly and depends in each case on state law. Generally, however, it may be said that libelous statements are conditionally privileged where facts exist, or are reasonably believed to exist, that cast on the author of the statement the duty to tell the public certain facts, and the author proceeds in good faith to do so. The defense of conditional privilege is lost when it is "abused" — where it can be shown that the statement was disseminated by a newspaper or broadcaster who knew it was false or who entertained serious doubts as to its truth.

Under most state laws, a newspaper or broadcaster has a conditional privilege to report fairly and accurately judicial or legislative proceedings, even though statements made in those proceedings are defamatory. The publication should merely report the official proceedings and the statements made by the participants. The newspaper or broadcaster must be certain that the report is full, fair, impartial, and accurate, and it must not seriously doubt the truth of the accusations.

Journalistic shorthand shouldn't summarize complicated proceedings if the result is to make the report unfair or inaccurate.

For example, where statements concerning the guilt or innocence of an arrested party are made by coroners, detectives, or other public officers acting as witnesses at a judicial proceeding, a full, fair, impartial, and accurate report of such statements is privileged, even though the statements eventually turn out to be false and defamatory. On the other hand, if it can be proved that the reporter independently had information that made him or her have serious doubts as to the truth of such statements, then the privilege may be jeopardized. Neither are such statements privileged if made outside judicial proceedings by the public officers.

In general, the conditional privilege applies to all proceedings that are judicial in nature, from preliminary hearings before a justice of the peace to arguments in the Supreme Court. The privilege also applies to many quasi-judicial proceedings, such as coroners' inquests and reports of grand juries, and to reports of proceedings and investigations of legislative bodies. It does not apply to proceedings of a distinctly private nature.

Accurate reports of official public records and documents to which the public has a right of access are conditionally privileged. In fact, some states have statutes which enumerate in considerable detail the kinds of proceedings and records that are protected as privileged communications.

Opinion and fair comment

It is axiomatic that only misstatements of fact can serve as the basis for a libel suit. Thus, libel plaintiffs invariably try to persuade judges that the libelous remark reasonably implied false facts about them. Conversely, the defendants in libel actions seek to have the remarks categorized as opinion, for if they succeed, they will have two defenses among their arsenal: (1) a federal constitutional defense, and (2) a common law defense of fair comment.

The line between fact and opinion is often hazy, but there are guideposts. Verifiability is crucial; can a statement be proved true or false? The overall tenor or context of the statement will be looked at to see if it negates the impression that the statement is factual. But phrasing can be determinative. Describing a steakhouse's meat as 'less than prime' could be seen as a statement of fact, while complaining that it 'tasted like shoe leather' would be pure opinion. Perhaps the single most important rule simply reflects a tenet of good journalism: **When expressing an opinion, set forth the facts on which you base your view and then state your opinion.**

Political debate can ignite fireworks of charges and countercharges, many of them classifiable as opinion rather than fact. Often courts will speak of such "lusty and imaginative expressions" as rhetorical hyperbole, not meant to be taken as literally true. Thus, such terms as "blackmailer," "scab," "sleazy," "jerk," and "fascist" have been held to be nonactionable opinion in certain contexts.

The state law defense of fair comment varies somewhat in each jurisdiction but fundamentally protects criticism — no matter how caustic or incredible — if the following elements are present:

a. The comment or criticism must be on a matter of public interest.

b. The comment or criticism must be based upon certain facts which are fully stated and are believed to be true.

c. The comment or criticism must be purely comment or criticism and not an allegation of fact. Statements lose the protection granted to opinion when they imply that they are based on certain undisclosed, libelous facts. Thus, if you write "Senator Pegleg is an alcoholic" without basing that view on your factual observation of the senator consuming five martinis as regular luncheon fare, you may have stated an assertion, not an opinion.

Readers must receive a true and clear picture of the conduct condemned and be able to separate the comment or criticism from the facts on which that comment or criticism is based.

d. The comment or criticism must not be malicious. Comment or criticism is always impersonal. A commentator or critic has no right to take advantage of an occasion to gratify any private grudge or to seek any end other than a fair discussion of matters of public interest.

Consent

A person who authorizes, requests, induces, or otherwise consents to the publication of matter about himself or herself takes the risk that it is or may be defamatory. A newspaper or broadcaster, then, is privileged to publish libelous matter if the person libeled consents to it.

The terms of the consent determine the extent of the privilege, however. On the rare occasions when the consent can reasonably be interpreted to give assent to the publication of libel to any person at any time in any manner and for any purpose, the publication is unrestricted and absolutely privileged. More often, the consent is conditioned upon a certain contingency or limited to a particular time or for a particular purpose. Accordingly, the defense of consent is lost where the publication goes beyond the scope of those conditions or limitations.

Consent may be explicit, implied, or apparent from words or other conduct that, in light of the surrounding circumstances, may be reasonably interpreted as assent. For instance, implied consent to a defamatory publication may be obtained by requesting and receiving from the person defamed a voluntary affirmative and detailed answer to it; but his mere denial, refusal to answer, or silence concerning the charge does not constitute consent. Similarly, a person may consent to an original defamatory report without necessarily consenting to any repetition of it.

The right of reply

The defense of the right of reply may be likened to self-defense. That is, a person has the right to defend himself or herself against the attack of another not only by rebuffing the attack but also by pursuing an affirmative counterattack in an effort to negate, compromise, or discourage the attack.

Generally, a publication or broadcast that in good faith and without malice seeks to defend against an attack upon the character, interests, or activities of any person or entity is qualifiedly privileged, even though that publication or broadcast is false and defamatory. However, the reply must be reasonably pertinent to and not exceed the scope of the attack. For example, a newspaper, at the request of one political candidate who has been attacked by another, has a qualified privilege to publish a defamatory reply, so long as the reply is published in good faith, bears a reasonable relationship to the attack, and does not surpass the attack in magnitude.

Statute of limitations

A cause of action for libel ordinarily accrues from the time of first publication or broadcast. Moreover, to prevent a multiplicity of lawsuits, it is generally recognized that a single issue of a newspaper, although widely distributed, or a single broadcast constitutes only one publication and one cause of action. The statute of limitations runs from the date of that first publication, and any libel action thereon must be commenced before the time fixed by statute has expired. Otherwise, the action is barred.

Statutes of limitation for libel vary from state to state, generally ranging from one to three years after accrual of the cause of action. A publisher or broadcaster should be aware of the statute of limitations of each state in which his newspaper or broadcast material is disseminated. Recent court decisions have ruled that journalists can be sued in states other than their home states under many circumstances.

MITIGATING CIRCUMSTANCES

In general

In addition to the six defenses previously described, there are certain "partial" defenses to a libel action that are really not defenses at all and are used only to minimize the damages awarded in a libel trial. Unlike the complete defenses of truth, privilege, opinion and fair comment, consent, the right of reply, and the statute of limitations, they do not completely bar recovery of damages.

Generally, partial defenses serve only to mitigate damages by showing the absence of ill will on the part of the defendant or the general bad character and reputation of the plaintiff. They may be of faint or no comfort in a lawsuit.

Many states have provided by statute for pleading and proving mitigating circumstances to reduce damages. Therefore, the laws of each state should be consulted to determine the extent to which any partial defenses may be applicable.

Retraction

A retraction, correction, or apology for a published libel is not a defense to a libel action, but may serve to mitigate damages. As a practical matter, a retraction may avert a libel action altogether by adequately pacifying and appeasing the defamed person. In the event of a lawsuit, a retraction affords proof of lack of ill will and may substantially atone for any injury to a plaintiff's character or reputation.

All demands for retractions, especially when made by a lawyer for a potential plaintiff, should be handled with the advice of legal counsel. A well-meaning correction may actually put a publisher or broadcaster in a worse position in a subsequent lawsuit. For example, a badly worded clarification of an ambiguous story may tacitly concede what a plaintiff would otherwise have to prove.

To date, thirty-three states have statutes specifically providing for the retraction of a libel. These states are Alabama, Arizona, California, Connecticut, Florida, Georgia, Idaho, Indiana, Iowa, Kentucky, Maine, Massachusetts, Michigan, Minnesota, Mississippi, Montana, Nebraska, Nevada, New Jersey, North Carolina, North Dakota, Ohio, Oklahoma, Oregon, South Dakota, Tennessee, Texas, Utah, Virginia, Washington, West Virginia, Wisconsin, and Wyoming. The other seventeen states, Puerto Rico, and the District of Columbia make no statutory provision for retraction but generally permit the introduction of evidence of a retraction in mitigation of damages.

A typical retraction statute requires a plaintiff, within a

definite time, to demand a retraction before he is entitled to more than actual or special damages. Thereafter, the defendant is given a certain time to publish a retraction. If the defendant makes a timely retraction (and under many statutes also shows that the original report was made in good faith), the plaintiff is normally limited to a recovery of compensatory damages only. On the other hand, if the defendant does not make a timely retraction, the plaintiff may be entitled to recover punitive damages as well as compensatory damages, provided he can prove that the libel was made with knowledge of its falsity or with serious doubts as to its truth.

Mistaken identity

A newspaper or broadcaster may not successfully claim as a defense a mistake or ambiguity in the name or description of a party referred to in a libelous report. A plaintiff is entitled to recover if those reading or hearing the libelous story reasonably understood that it referred to the plaintiff, even though the newspaper or broadcaster intended to refer to someone else. In such cases, the law disregards innocent motive and intent on the part of the newspaper or broadcaster, and it protects the party actually harmed by holding the newspaper or broadcaster responsible for any mistake or ambiguity in the identity of that party. As a result, the newspaper or broadcaster may avoid damages only by showing that the mistake or ambiguity was inadvertent and free from negligence or, in the case of public persons, reckless disregard of the truth.

Provocation

Where a reply to an attack is not relative to or exceeds the scope of the attack, the complete defense of the right of reply is not available to the defendant. Nevertheless, it may be possible for the defendant at least to mitigate punitive damages by interposing the partial defense of provocation. Hence, it may be shown in mitigation of damages that the excessively passionate and defamatory report was directly and proximately prompted by the nearly concurrent provocative attack of the plaintiff.

Bad character of plaintiff

A plaintiff is entitled to recover damages for harm done to his character and reputation. It is possible, however, that his previous character and reputation were so notoriously bad that he could not be damaged by any new defamation, even though undeserved. Accordingly, proof that a plaintiff's general character and reputation in the community and in relation to the matter charged were already bad at or before the time of the libel may be considered by a jury in mitigation of damages. Frequently, only nominal damages are awarded in such cases.

The "libel-proof" defense

During the last decade, some courts have recognized that the nature of a particular libel may be so inconsequential in relation to the plaintiff's already terrible reputation that the newspaper or broadcaster should have a complete defense to a libel action. These courts speak of the plaintiff's being "libel-proof." Persons such as convicted assassins or other nefarious types may, under this theory, be so devoid of reputation that they could not maintain any libel action except one predicated on a deliberate fabrication. This emerging "libel-proof" defense cannot be relied upon to make all convicts or other poorly regarded people "fair game." The defense will likely be more useful to defense attorneys than in assessing risks prior to publication or broadcast.

PROTECTING CONFIDENTIAL SOURCES

Sources and newsroom discussions

Once a suit for libel or invasion of privacy has been instituted, the plaintiff may attempt to discover evidence demonstrating that the publisher or broadcaster acted with the requisite degree of fault. Often, the plaintiff will call upon the power of the court to compel a defendant to disclose the identity of sources, interview notes, "outtakes," or the content of "editorial discussions" within the newsroom.

The U.S. Supreme Court has held that the press enjoys no constitutional privilege to withhold information about the "editorial process"; i.e., those newsroom discussions about the "angle" pursued in a story, the emphasis of a lead or headline, the selection of quotations from sources, or the reliability of certain sources. Libel plaintiffs will often explore the editorial process in the hope of discovering evidence that the reporters acted negligently or in fact entertained serious doubts about the truth of what they were publishing or broadcasting.

Disclosing sources and disgorging material used to prepare a story can present ethical dilemmas for reporters in a libel case. On the one hand, they want to win the libel suit and vindicate their editorial integrity; on the other, they do not want to jeopardize their newsgathering ability by breaking promises of confidentiality to sources. Unsurprisingly, therefore, protecting sources has become the bloodiest terrain on the battlefield of libel litigation in recent years.

The press has experienced mixed success in withholding the identity of sources, notes, and outtakes from libel plaintiffs. Successes have been based on either (a) the presence of state shield laws or (b) a reporter's "conditional" First Amendment privilege to refuse to disclose such information. This First Amendment privilege is recognized by most jurisdictions but it is not absolute and may be overcome when the libel plaintiff can demonstrate (1) the relevance of the information sought, (2) the unavailability of the information from alternative sources, and (3) a "compelling" need of some sort. Typically, courts will not find a compelling need unless (a) there is already other evidence that the publisher or broadcaster is at fault and (b) the defendant is the only known source of the alleged libel.

State shield laws, particularly the "unqualified" shield laws—such as Ohio's or Pennsylvania's, which contain no exceptions—have also been extremely useful to the press in resisting disclosure of confidential sources.

The consequences of refusing to comply with a judicial disclosure order are onerous indeed. Noncompliance can result in an instruction to a jury that a refusal to reveal a source for the libelous story creates the presumption that there is no source. Courts also retain the power to incarcerate a reporter or editor who disobeys a judicial order.

Notes and memos: record retention

Reporters are often shocked, once a libel lawsuit has begun, to learn that a plaintiff is entitled to obtain copies of their notes, internal memos to editors, and all other written or taped records relating to the lawsuit. There are exceptions to this rule that exclude, for instance, records subject to the attorney-client privilege or records revealing a confidential source. But, generally, the paper trail (or tape trail) leading to publication or broadcast of a story may be obtained by a plaintiff. Moreover, reporters are frequently subpoenaed to produce notes about matters they've investigated for use in other kinds of litigation, and such subpoenas can embroil the reporter in a legal tug of war over notes.

Most reporters take notes and write memos to assist them in doing their jobs, not to prepare or protect themselves for the remote possibility of future litigation. Thus, most reporters' notebooks may be personally useful but subject to being distorted or unfairly characterized by plaintiffs' lawyers in litigation. It is for this reason (and to avoid hassles with third party subpoenas) that many defense lawyers advise reporters to routinely destroy all notes and records for which they do not have a specific identifiable need. This flexible record retention policy permits reporters to preserve records that may be helpful as background for future stories or, for that matter, as corroborating evidence of either a source's consent to be interviewed or his actual statements. When in doubt whether to retain records, reporters should consult with their editors since policies differ widely and sometimes vary depending upon the particular records involved.

INVASION OF PRIVACY

IN GENERAL

The right of privacy is closely related to the law of libel. Frequently, a single publication will provide the basis for actions for both libel and invasion of the right of privacy. The fundamental difference between the two actions is that, whereas the law of libel protects primarily a person's character and reputation, the right of privacy protects primarily a person's peace of mind, spirit, sensibilities, and feelings.

The other major difference is that libel always involves falsity but invasion of privacy may involve the disclosure of truth.

Invasion of privacy was not recognized as a tort under common law and, accordingly, was not inherited from England. Instead, just before the turn of the century, the right of privacy started to develop in this country as the result of an influential law review article published by then-attorney, later Supreme Court justice, Louis D. Brandeis. In the ensuing decades, more and more states have recognized some variant of the right of privacy, protecting the right of a person to be free from unwarranted and unauthorized exposure of his or her person or of those personal affairs in which the public has no legitimate interest.

In simple terms, then, the right of privacy is the right of a person to be "let alone" to enjoy life as he or she sees fit, without his or her name, visage, or activities becoming public property, unless he or she waives or relinquishes this right.

The right of privacy is a personal right protecting the feelings and sensibilities of living persons only. Thus, for example, corporations and public institutions have no right of privacy, barring a statute to the contrary. As a general rule, this personal right of privacy is not relational and dies with the person, although some courts recognize the rights of heirs of such celebrities as Elvis Presley or Humphrey Bogart to control the commercial exploitation of the dead person. Usually, however, relatives of deceased persons suffer no invasion of their right of privacy from any grief or embarrassment caused by publicity concerning the deceased.

THE RIGHT OF PRIVACY

Most states that have had occasion to consider an alleged invocation of the right of privacy have recognized the right by judicial decisions or statutes.

Generally, a person's privacy can be invaded in one of the following ways:

1. **Intrusion** — by unreasonably intruding, physically or otherwise, upon the solitude or seclusion of another, or in that person's private affairs or concerns. Actual publication of information is irrelevant to a claim of "intrusion."

   Rather, this type of invasion of privacy is associated with newsgathering and usually involves the wrongful use of tape recorders, microphones, cameras, and other electronic recording or eavesdropping devices to record a person's private activities. It is likely to occur if a reporter misrepresents himself to gain access to a place or person or trespasses upon private property. In Jacqueline Onassis's suit against photographer Ron Galella, the court found that his constant interferences with her daily life constituted "intrusion." Likewise, television stations have lost intrusion cases when cameramen trespassed on a public utility's land in order to film trespassing demonstrators against nuclear power.

   Courts have resisted efforts to find intrusion when the press receives confidential documents purloined by a third party. The general rule, according to one court, is that a newspaper does not commit intrusion by its "mere receipt" of illegally obtained documents, "even when the newspaper has actual knowledge of such impropriety." If the newspaper takes some part in the illegal act, however, a suit for "intrusion" may be successful.

2. **Publicizing private matter** — by publicizing a matter concerning the private life of a person which would offend ordinary sensibilities.

   Sensational disclosures about a person's health, sexual activity, social or economic affairs, and other private matters are examples of this type of invasion of privacy. These disclosures must concern private facts. A press report about, or a photograph of, an event that takes place in public, no matter how sensational or embarrassing, is not actionable. Thus, the press can't be sued for displaying a photograph of teenagers kissing or a laborer playing hooky on a public street. As long as the camera records only what the naked eye could see in public, there should be no actionable invasion.

3. **Publicizing in a false light** — by publicizing a matter concerning a person that places the person before the public in a "false light." This type of invasion of privacy is closely akin to libel since it also involves the element of falsity.

   The invasion most commonly occurs when reporters attempt to condense or fictionalize in an effort to write a dramatic news or feature story. It has become increasingly prominent in recent years with the advent of television "docudramas" or novels that are thinly disguised biographies. Although courts have held that the incidental, non-defamatory use of an actual person's name in a fictionalized account is not actionable, wholesale creation of a fictional character who closely resembles a living person may lead to liability. Photographs that accompany "soft news" or features stories are another fertile source of "false light" claims, especially when a story describes uncomplimentary events that do not pertain to the persons pictured. Most courts will absolve a defendant in such a case in the absence of evidence that it intended to create a false impression.

4. **Appropriation** — by appropriating a person's name, likeness or personality for advertising or commercial purposes or for one's own use or benefit.

   This type of invasion of privacy is derived from a long-standing New York statute that expressly prohibits the use of a person's name or likeness for advertising or trade purposes without written consent. Generally, New York and other states have held that a newspaper or broadcaster may use the name or picture of a person without his consent in connection with current or even past news events and biographies of legitimate public interest.

However, many entertainers, sports personalities, and other celebrities jealously guard the commercial exploitation of their name, picture and performances. Some state courts refer to this as the "right of publicity." Accordingly, editors and news producers should be careful with feature stories that essentially appropriate or exploit the commercial value of a person.

DEFENSES

The right of privacy can be waived or relinquished in various ways:

1. **Consent:** A person may expressly consent to an invasion of privacy. Consent, of course, is rarely obtainable, feasible, or really necessary in the case of a newspaper or broadcaster that reports countless names and pictures of those who make the news daily. Moreover, even consent in writing can usually be conditioned, revoked, or withdrawn at will. It is essential to obtain consent and a release, however, in the case of advertising or other commercial use of a person's name, likeness or personality.

2. **Newsworthiness** — public figures: The name or picture of a public official or public figure can be used without that person's consent in a noncommercial context. In recent years, courts have used the definitions of public figures and public officials formulated in the libel context in suits alleging invasion of privacy. The rationale appears to be that a public figure invites public interest and must accept even unwelcome publicity. Even the private life of such a public figure may be publicized without the individual's consent to the extent legitimately necessary and proper in dealing with the public figure's activities of public concern. Moreover, the public has a continuing interest in a public figure even after retirement from public life. Therefore, the public

figure is generally subject to, and cannot complain of, unauthorized reports concerning past fame.

3. **Newsworthiness** — private individuals: The law of privacy, unlike defamation, recognizes a defense whenever a publication concerns a matter of "public interest."

   Thus, the unauthorized publication or broadcast of the name or picture of a private citizen who becomes a participant, unwilling or otherwise, in a newsworthy occurrence of legitimate interest to the public is not an invasion of privacy. For, unexpectedly or involuntarily, any private citizen may become an object of legitimate news interest to the public, either as an individual (such as a victim, villain, or hero of a newsworthy occurrence) or as a member of a group of persons participating in, or fortuitously present at, a news event. Accordingly, courts have held that much arguably private material is of legitimate public interest, including the grades of college athletes and the identities of rape victims, drug addicts, and unnecessarily sterilized women.

   Nevertheless, the unwarranted and unauthorized exposure of the private affairs of a private citizen, which is offensive to ordinary sensibilities and which has no legitimate interest to the public, invades his or her right of privacy. Generally, a jury decides whether such unauthorized reports are news events of legitimate public interest.

   Theoretically, even a report on a matter of public record — such as the sale of a residence or an arrest — could invade a person's privacy if the report also contains gratuitous private matters about the person that offend ordinary sensibilities. But the U.S. Supreme Court has held that accurate reports of the contents of court and police records, such as the identity of a rape victim, cannot constitute an invasion of privacy.

4. **Constitutional privilege:** Newspapers and broadcasters have the defense of a constitutional privilege to the "false light" type of invasion of privacy. In a "false light" case, a person involved in a matter of public interest cannot recover damages unless the individual can prove that the newspaper or broadcaster made the statement knowing it was false or entertaining serious doubts as to its truth. This defense is

akin to, and derived from, the constitutional proof requirements for public officials and public figures in libel law.

It is also settled constitutional law that truthful publications concerning matters of public interest, although private, are not subject to liability for invasion of privacy. The U.S. Supreme Court has held that "the defense of truth is constitutionally required where the subject of the publication is a public official or public figure." It is unclear, however, whether all truthful publications are protected by the First Amendment.

MITIGATION

In addition to these three defenses, a newspaper or broadcaster may mitigate damages by showing the plaintiff's oral consent or course of conduct indicating consent to the publication about which the complaint has been drawn. However, neither the absence of malice nor good motives prompting a report about a person constitute defenses to a subsequent action for invasion of privacy. Likewise, where a report does in fact invade a plaintiff's right of privacy, it is generally no defense that the person's name or picture was used by mistake, inadvertence, or in a justified, but mistaken, belief that the report had been authorized by the plaintiff.

"RED FLAG" WORDS

The following selected "red flag" words and expressions typify the numerous words and expressions that may lead to a libel lawsuit if not carefully handled in news stories.

A

addict
adulteration of products
adultery
AIDS
alcoholic
altered records
atheist

B

bad moral character
bankrupt
bigamist
blacklisted
blackmail
booze-hound
bribery
brothel
buys votes

C

cheats
child abuse
collusion
con artist
confidence man
corruption
coward
crook

D

deadbeat
defaulter
divorced
double-crosser
drug abuser
drunkard

E

ex-convict

F

fawning sycophant
fraud

G

gambling den
gangster

gay
graft
groveling office seeker

H

herpes
hit-man
hypocrite

I

illegitimate
illicit relation
incompetent
infidelity
informer
insider trading
intemperate
intimate
intolerance

J

Jekyll-Hyde personality

K

kept woman
Ku Klux Klan

M

Mafia
mental illness
mobster
moral delinquency
mouthpiece

N

Nazi

P

paramour

peeping Tom
perjurer
plagiarist
pockets public funds
profiteering
prostitute

S

scam
scandalmonger
scoundrel
seducer
sharp dealing
shyster
slacker
smooth and tricky
smuggler
sneaky
sold influence
sold out
spy
stool pigeon
stuffed the ballot box
suicide
swindle

T

thief

U

unethical
unmarried mother
unprofessional
unsound mind
unworthy of credit

V

vice den
villain

Any words or expressions imputing:

a loathsome disease;

a crime, or words falsely charging arrest or indictment for or confession or conviction of a crime;

anti-Semitism or other religious, racial or ethnic intolerance;

connivance or association with criminals;

financial embarrassment (or any implication of insolvency or want of credit);

lying;

membership in an organization which may be in disrepute at a given time;

poverty or squalor;

unwillingness to pay a debt.

ABOUT THE AUTHOR

BRUCE W. SANFORD is a partner with the Washington office of Baker & Hostetler and a widely-recognized authority on communications law and the American media. The *Washington Journalism Review* has termed him "one of the most accomplished press lawyers" in the nation.

Mr. Sanford serves as general counsel to the Society of Professional Journalists, the largest and oldest organization of journalists in the United States, and has represented such national news media as Scripps Howard, The New York Times, The Chicago Sun-Times, Independent Newspapers, Inc., The Hearst Corporation, CBS, Inc., Gannett Co., Inc., Time Warner, Inc., William Morrow & Co., Bantam Books, and Avon Books in a wide range of libel and other First Amendment matters. He is a member of the bars of New York, Ohio, Maryland and the District of Columbia, and has consulted on libel matters in England, Canada, Hong Kong and other countries.

A *cum laude* graduate of Hamilton College, Mr. Sanford is a former intern of Dow Jones' The Newspaper Fund and worked as a staff reporter for *The Wall Street Journal* prior to attending law school. He earned his Juris Doctor degree at New York University's School of Law.

During his career, Mr. Sanford has defended more than 800 libel and related cases throughout the United States and abroad. His other work in communications law focuses on FCC regulation of broadcasters and common carriers, prepublication counseling, and the defense of litigation involving privacy, prior restraints, subpoenas of newspersons, and rights of access to courtrooms and other public places and information. On Capitol Hill, he has testified frequently on the Freedom of Information Act, the Fairness Doctrine and other content regulation of electronic media or national security matters.

He is the author of *Libel and Privacy*, a 900-page treatise for lawyers and editors, the second edition of which will be published in 1991 by Prentice Hall. A contributor to the *Columbia Journalism Review*, *The Quill,* and the *Washington Journalism Review,* and instructor at the American Press Institute, he has written and spoken widely on the practical effects of modern libel and privacy law for working journalists.

He is the Chairman of the Board of Trustees of The Thomas Jefferson Center for the Protection of Free Expression at the University of Virginia.